I SURVIVED IT
THE REBIRTH

CHANEL LANDRY

Disclaimer

This book is based on true events. Some names and identifying details may have been changed to protect privacy. The information shared is for inspirational and educational purposes only and should not be considered medical, legal, or professional advice. Readers should consult qualified professionals regarding any decisions related to their health or personal circumstances.

Preface

You see the beauty, but not the ashes. The home, the career, the businesses, and the smile you see today came at a cost. Behind every blessing is a battle I had to survive.

This book is my testimony. It is not just about the pain I endured, but the healing, forgiveness, and faith that carried me through. I Survived It: The Rebirth is my journey of rising from brokenness to wholeness, from silence to speaking life, and from surviving to truly living.

I wrote these pages to remind you that you are not alone. Whatever you have faced loss, trauma, disappointment, or heartbreak you, too, can rise again. My hope is that as you read my story, you will find pieces of your own, and that these words will ignite your courage to heal, grow, and step into your rebirth.

This is more than my story it's a reflection of God's grace, a reminder of His power to restore, and a call to never give up.

James 1 1:2-3 NIV
Consider it pure joy my brothers and sisters, whenever you face trials of many kinds, because you know that the testing of your faith produces perseverance. Let perseverance finish its work so that you may mature and complete, not lacking anything.

With love and gratitude,
Chanel Landry, BSN, RN

Acknowlegements

First and foremost, I give thanks to God for granting me the strength, wisdom, clarity, determination and perseverance to write this book. Without his guidance, this journey would not have been possible. It is through Him that I found the courage to share my story.

This book is dedicated to my grandparents, R.L. and A.L. I appreciate all the love you've shown me. Grandma, I miss you dearly and wish you were here to share in my accomplishments.

Secondly, to my parents without you, there would be no me. Thank you for making the best decisions for me. I love both of you. Last but not least, to my beautiful daughter, family and close friends who have supported me in all my endeavors. I extend my sincere thanks to my friend for carefully proofreading and thoughtful feedback that strengthen this book. A heartfelt thank you to Vernica Pitcher, my editor and illustrator, and Kimberly Neptune for contributing to my book. I am truly grateful for your time, talent, and support.

I love you all from the bottom of my heart.

Precious Memories

We all have cherished memories from childhood old photos, stories, friends, and beloved toys. I just experienced a flashback while looking at a photo from my Head Start graduation. I remember it vividly, as if it happened yesterday.

My aunt styled my hair into adorable Shirley Temple curls, and I wore a cute dress. After the ceremony, my dad and I took a photo together. Now, let's fast forward to the next stage of my life.

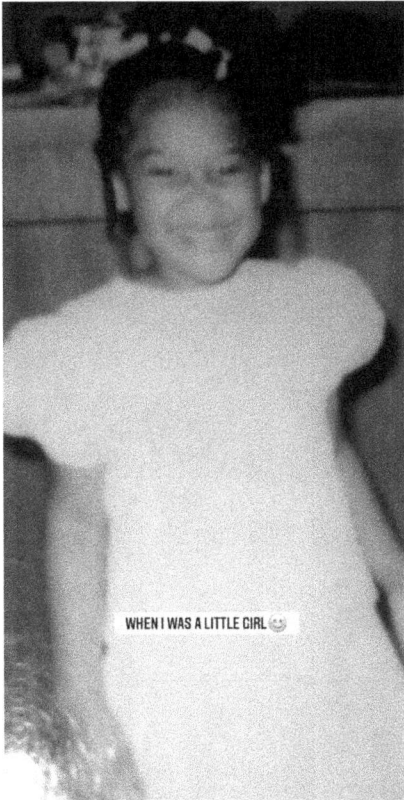

WHEN I WAS A LITTLE GIRL 😊

The Transition Detachment

Oh, boy, it's time to start kindergarten, but this year is different. Instead of starting the school year with my mom, I am now living with my paternal grandparents. They have spoiled me rotten; I never wanted for anything.

Raised in the Baptist church, my grandma sang in the choir, and my grandfather was a deacon. We were taught respect and always shown love, with the emphasis on putting God first, then family. Unfortunately, at this stage in my life, I struggled to express my true feelings and emotions.

At this stage in my life I was emotionally detached and too young to understand my mental state. I can imagine you're curious about my parents. We'll explore that later, so stay tuned!

■ The Transition Detachment - Reader Reflection

Think back to a time when life shifted suddenly moving homes, changing schools, or being raised by someone new. How did it shape you?

The Loss of Innocence

My innocence was taken during my elementary years when a family member exploited me. I experienced sexual molestation and felt too terrified to speak out until one day when Oprah aired a special on television. Various individuals shared their stories, which inspired me to confide in my family the next day about what I had endured. They responded appropriately, ensuring my protection from any further incidents and shielding me from the aggressor.

I am grateful to God for my family. Sadly, many children face blame, are not listened to, or they are told to keep such experiences secret. For a long time during my teenage years, only a few close family members were aware of what happened to me. I kept it bottled up, never discussing it with friends or anyone else.

■ The Loss of Innocence - Reader Reflection

If you've ever carried a secret pain, how did it feel to finally release it or what would it feel like if you could?

_____

_____

_____

_____

_____

_____

School In The 90's

(The Nostalgia of Youth: A Carefree Time)

Ah, the good old days filled with joy and free of worries. What a wonderful time it was! Academically, I thrived in school, often making the principal's list and even the superintendent's list at times. I was actively involved in numerous clubs, such as 4H, the Louisiana Technology Student Association, cheerleading, Beta, and more. I forged many lasting friendships, some of which I still cherish today. During high school, I was on a journey of self-discovery, blossoming into a young woman.

In my senior year, I had the honor of being on the homecoming court. Although I didn't win a title, it was an enriching experience overall. On the surface, everything in my life seemed to be going well, yet deep down, I felt a sense of emptiness as if something was missing. I knew what it was, but I kept it to myself.

■ School in the 90s - Reader Reflection

What's one school memory that shaped who you became, for better or for worse?

_____

_____

_____

_____

_____

_____

_____

Grownish

When I was a child, I dreamed of becoming a pediatrician. However, as I grew older, my aspirations shifted. I realized the lengthy amount of time I would spend in school and removed that goal from my list entirely. My first year of college marked my journey toward independence, during which I worked as a cashier at Walmart. This job lasted for a year until I chose to quit in order to focus on my studies full-time.

After about a year of balancing work and school, I decided to concentrate solely on my education. Nursing has always been my major, but I knew I needed to complete the required prerequisites, such as Sociology, Microbiology, and Anatomy, before applying for clinical.

Who would have thought that a Psychology class could lead to such personal liberation? One day, my psychology teacher assigned us to write a paper about our lives. I detailed my journey from the beginning to the present, I mean it was an incredible release! I felt free, unashamed, and deeply relieved. Everything I kept bottled up was finally out. From that moment on, I found the courage to speak openly about my molestation with others, and it no longer affected me. Sharing my story has been instrumental in helping many others.

It truly amazes me that when I share my story, others feel encouraged to open up and reveal they've had similar childhood experiences. Although the individuals involved may differ be it a relative, friend, or someone else I am grateful that I can remind them to stay strong. It's important for them to know that it's not their fault and that things will improve. God loves them and encourages them to never give up.

Forgiveness Heals

Focus on forgiving those who have wronged you. Remember, forgiveness is essential for your healing, freedom, and ability to truly live again. If you're reading this and have experienced molestation, rape, or any form of abuse, I encourage you to speak up.

Don't keep those feelings bottled up inside. Seek out a therapist, counselor, or someone you feel comfortable confiding in. Alternatively, writing down your thoughts might be a helpful outlet for you.

■ Forgiveness Heals - Reader Reflection

Is there someone you need to forgive not for them, but for your healing? Write about what forgiveness might mean for you.

Transitions

Reflecting on my experience at Louisiana Technical College fills me with joy as I recall the wonderful memories I made there. We were fortunate to have remarkable teachers, and I built many lasting friendships, with some of these friends becoming like sisters to me. During this time, I acquired invaluable knowledge and life lessons. A heartfelt thank you to my professors, including Dr. Leah Cullins, Arissa Grizzle, and Dawone Marshall, among others!

Despite the changes, I proudly graduated as an LPN in August 2005. I was thrilled and prepared to take my state board exam. However, that didn't go as planned. Hurricane Katrina hit, and it was such a shocking and chaotic experience. Many things were devastated, and tragically, lives were lost.

I began my journey with the Department of Children and Family Services. Due to interruptions in the system, I was unable to take my test until December. This catastrophic event is one we will never forget. My heartfelt condolences go out to all those who lost their lives and to everyone mourning family members. Once I passed my state boards, I was able to start working. I took on full-time shifts, overtime, and occasionally worked 12-hour days.

One day, while in a patient's room, I noticed a special on TV the St. Jude Marathon. My heart was touched by the incredible support they provided to children and families, all at no cost to them. Since that day in 2005, I have proudly been a donor to St. Jude. After passing my boards and putting in so much effort, I was finally able to reap the rewards of my hard work. I got the brand-new car I had always dreamed of: a sleek two-door black Honda coupe. After finishing nursing school, I felt I truly deserved the blessings that God had granted me.

The Miscarriage

Work and life were going wonderfully when, to my surprise, I discovered that a little blessing was on its way. I was overwhelmed with a whirlwind of emotions nervousness, shock, joy, and fear. My boyfriend and I shared the news with a few close friends, and within hours, my entire world flipped upside down. We learned I was pregnant on a Friday. However, by Saturday, I began spotting, and by Sunday, I found myself at the Emergency Department.

I was put on bed rest until Monday. During my first OBGYN appointment that Monday, I received the heartbreaking news that I was experiencing a miscarriage. The doctor conducted tests that revealed my pregnancy hormone levels were low and declining from the results obtained at the ER the day before. Then came the ultrasound, where, sadly, no heartbeat was detected, leaving me utterly devastated.

The doctor informed me that it was too soon for a dilation and curettage a procedure that entails opening the cervix and removing tissue from within the uterus. He advised me to let the miscarriage unfold naturally and promised to prescribe some medication for the pain. As a strong believer with faith in God, I accepted the prescription but chose not to take the medication, holding on to hope and refusing to accept his report.

I believed that God could change the situation and chose to ignore the doctor's prognosis. However, it was not part of God's plan, and His will prevailed. When I tell you, the pain I experienced was unbearable... far worse than labor pains.

At this moment, I want to reach out to any mother who has faced a similar situation filled with excitement for motherhood, only to have it cut short before experiencing it fully.

My heart goes out to you. I understand the pain; stay strong. Things will improve. Keep your faith, and when the time is right, God will bless you again if it aligns with his will.

I often found myself triggered by something as simple as a baby appearing in a TV commercial, leading me to cry in private. I never opened up about my feelings to my family; after all, I am typically seen as the strong one, the "no-limit soldier," who never shows vulnerability. Yet, inside, I was hurting. Witnessing others with their children made me reflect on what I had lost and the experiences we could have shared. The situation felt even more poignant as many of my friends and family were either pregnant or had just welcomed new babies, reminding me of my own loss constantly.

It's important to express your feelings openly; don't keep them bottled up. Share your emotions with your spouse, partner, or significant other, as they have feelings too. Even if they aren't the ones carrying the child, this experience affects them deeply. Often, men and even children may struggle to articulate their feelings.

Your kids might be eager to become a big brother or sister, but they may also be grappling with the reality of having an angel instead. Engage with them at their level to help them understand what has happened. I am truly grateful for the strength I've found throughout this experience; I could have easily lost my composure or faced a breakdown, but thankfully, I didn't.

■ The Miscarriage - Reader Reflection

When have you experienced a loss that others couldn't fully see or understand? How did you find strength to go on?

Rainbow Baby

After the rain, the sun will shine once more. I am deeply grateful, Lord, for the blessing of my smart and beautiful baby girl. She means everything to me and so much more. She is my reason for everything; my motivation to work hard, rise each day, and keep pushing forward.

Be patient; when the time is right, God will bless you according to His will. I still find it hard to believe that I am a mother, and this year, I will celebrate my child turning 18 and starting college.

■ Rainbow Baby - Reader Reflection

What blessing in your life came after a season of deep pain?

_____

_____

_____

_____

_____

_____

_____

_____

_____

_____

_____

The Loss of a Loved One

This experience was profoundly significant for me. I lost my everything; my grandmother, the woman who raised me, my adopted mother. She left this world to return home to the Lord, and it shook my entire world. Imagine going in for what you believe is a simple procedure, expecting to come home in one to two days, only to find yourself in the SICU and then the CCU. I will carry this memory with me for the rest of my life. The day before Thanksgiving, I spent time with her, preparing all the food. My aunt called, asking me to persuade her to reschedule her appointment, but she wouldn't listen; she was adamant about going through with the procedure.

Have you ever heard the saying that people know when it's their last day on Earth, yet they can't communicate it? You might reflect on small things they said after they're gone and realize, "Wow, that was a sign I overlooked." Little did we know she was already aware and at peace with her decision. She had even told a few people to look after her family. During this time, I had re-enrolled in nursing school to become a Registered Nurse, and I was in my junior year, specifically in my OBGYN rotation.

I remember it as if it were just yesterday, dozing off in the waiting room, anxiously awaiting updates from the doctors. Nearly everyday for a week, I moved between Woman's Hospital for OBGYN clinical and the ICU waiting room at OLOL. Sadly, we received the news we had dreaded: they would have to disconnect my grandma from life support, and it was time to bid her farewell. My final moments with her wow, I can still picture it vividly. The countless machines, medications, and tubes surrounding her; I have immense gratitude for the critical care nurses.

I recall whispering that I loved her and reassured her that we would be okay. In that moment, a single tear rolled down her cheek. As we walked back to the waiting area, my angel felt weary and peacefully went to rest with the Lord.

This experience felt so surreal; I hardly cried. I was focused on staying strong and holding it together for everyone else until we reached the cemetery. That was when the reality struck me, and I lost it. After that, everything became a blur until I opened my eyes and found myself in a car heading home.

One thing I know for sure is that the Lord was with me. How I managed to get through finals was purely by God's grace and the support of my classmates. A heartfelt shout-out to the OLOL nursing class crew for keeping me updated with my work. Their support was truly unmatched, and I cherish those ladies. This was an incredibly challenging time; I battled feelings of depression and stress and struggled to get any sleep. I would lie awake until dawn, feeling restless.

I experienced profound pain when she passed away. She never had the opportunity to share in the joyful moments with me after I completed my education. We often discussed how I would relocate and how she would come visit for fishing trips at my home. However, I am grateful that she did get to enjoy happy times with my daughter.

A year after her passing, I graduated from nursing school and earned my degree as a registered nurse. I want to take this moment to encourage anyone reading this to express your genuine feelings to your family and friends. Make sure to show and tell them you love them while they are still here with us. Once their eyes close for the last time, it becomes too late. I often find myself wishing I could turn back time to demonstrate how much I love and appreciate my grandma. Even after 14 years, it feels like just yesterday.

Now that I've matured, I understand more about life and its brevity, and I've learned not to take people and experiences for granted. There's always a song that brings back memories of someone special.

Whenever I hear "Let the Church Say Amen" by Andréa Crouch featuring Marvin Winans, I can't help but smile. That song played during our drive to the funeral. Indeed, God has spoken; let the church say amen.

■ The Loss of a Loved One - Reader Reflection

If you could say one more thing to someone you've lost, what would it be?

New Home, New Beginnings

It felt great to celebrate the rewards of my hard work and labor. I felt incredibly blessed to have acquired a brand-new house for my daughter and I. I was overflowing with gratitude, joy, and appreciation. I couldn't wait to create beautiful memories with my little angel. It marked a fresh start for us. It was truly a blessing to be in my twenties and have the ability to provide for my daughter. It is truly a blessing to be spending year 11 in our home. Thank you God.

■ New Home, New Beginnings - Reader Reflection

What does "home" mean to you not just the place, but the feeling?

Dating Again

Life was going wonderfully. I had a fulfilling career, a nice home, and everything seemed to be in place. It felt like the right time to start dating again, especially since my child's father and I had ended our relationship years ago. We were both young and evolving when we first got together, and it became clear that we were better off apart.

After a couple of years, I thought, "Why not explore the dating scene again?" I began seeing someone new, and for a while, everything seemed perfect. We enjoyed each other's company, going out on dates to the movies, shopping trips, restaurants, traveling, attending church, and more. However, I have a strong discerning spirit, and when I sense something, I trust my instincts.

Let's just say, when you pray and ask the Lord for clarity, be prepared for what you may uncover. As my grandma always said, "Whatever is done in the dark will come to light," and that saying holds true. While I acknowledge my own faults, there are certain things one cannot compromise on. So, for now, it looks like single life is the path I'll continue on.

I refuse to allow the actions of one person to shape my perception of others. I still believe in love; my ex simply wasn't the right match for me. It's essential for each of us to recognize our self-worth. You deserve to be loved in the right way. Set your standards high and don't tolerate less than you deserve.

Never settle just to claim you're in a relationship. Learn to love yourself first. Spend time dating yourself and prioritize healing before seeking a new partner. If you haven't healed, you may carry the same emotional baggage into your next relationship. As for me, I'm focusing on self-love and patiently waiting for God to bring the right man into my life. In the meantime, I'm going to travel, live, and savor every moment.

Fulfilling My Purpose

I have dedicated over 20 years to the nursing profession. While nursing certainly has its challenges, I am grateful that God has called me to care for and support others. My ambition is to advance my career and continue until I achieve the title of Dr. Landry.

Now, I want to take a moment to uplift you. Yes, you! It's never too late to finish what you've started. Revisit your goals and pursue that degree! It's possible that you chose your career path based on the expectations of your parents or others, like becoming a lawyer when really you wanted to be Physical Therapist.

Now is the moment to pursue what truly makes you happy. Don't continue to feel miserable and wake up each day burdened by regret. Life is too fleeting; seize the opportunity now. It doesn't matter if you're 70; you can still make it happen.

■ Fulfilling My Purpose - Reader Reflection

If you could revisit a dream you once had, what would it be? How could you take one step toward it now?

Entrepreneurship Is Not For The Weak

I understand that you might be tired of hearing this story, but please bear with me, as it's for those who are just getting to know me. I always aspired to be a business owner, but I was uncertain about which venture to pursue. After praying for guidance, I was led to the idea of starting a scrubs business. A quick search revealed that a store was located just two minutes away. However, some scrub retailers restrict sales within a 15-mile radius.

Thus, I decided to launch a fashion boutique named Paris and Paisley Boutique. With my passion for fashion, I focused on children's clothing, initially branding it as "A Fashion Closet for Kids." Before long, my store expanded to include women's fashion as well. This year marks our sixth anniversary, and I feel truly blessed; women from all over the U.S. have shopped with us, with our farthest customer residing in Canada. We are immensely grateful for this success.

■ Entrepreneurship Is Not for the Weak - Reader Reflection

What's one idea or passion you've always thought about turning into a business? What's holding you back?

Introducing, Nola Scrubs

A year after establishing Paris and Paisley Boutique, I ventured into a new project: Frontline Medical Scrubs and Accessories. Little did I know that a pandemic would bring unprecedented challenges. I aimed to trademark my business and elevate it further, but due to the widespread use of the term "frontline," I encountered hurdles. Someone even adopted my exact name.

As a result, we had to restart the process, leading to the rebranding of the store as Nola Scrubs. At Nola Scrubs, we offer comfortable, quality, accessories and fashionable scrubs, ensuring our customers look and feel great. We are growing by the day. Be on the lookout for what God has in store for us we will be known all over the world soon.

■ Introducing, Nola Scrubs - Reader Reflection

Have you ever felt led to start something new whether a business, ministry, or personal project that felt bigger than you? What steps can you take today to move closer to that vision?

2020: The Year the World Stopped

Pandemic – A pandemic (/pænˈdɛmɪk/ pan-DEM-ik) is defined as an outbreak of an infectious disease that has spread widely, affecting many people across multiple continents or globally. (Wikipedia)

This year was undeniably daunting and challenging, not just in the United States but all around the world. We were forced to bring our familiar way of life to a halt. In my role, we shifted to fully remote positions, working from home without any in-person interactions with providers or practices.

Medical professionals and frontline workers emerged as our heroes during this time. The impact of this disease was profound, affecting countless families. I experienced personal loss, beginning with my grandfather, followed by two aunts within the same week.
We had to wear masks and maintain social distance. We were unable to be with our loved ones during their moments of need or even while in the hospital. Funerals were transformed into something unrecognizable.

I vividly remember attending my grandfather's funeral in New Orleans, where we were spaced far apart. Only ten individuals were allowed inside, meaning even my grandfather's siblings could not attend. That was heart-wrenching. It felt surreal, as if I was living in a dream.
My uncle, who was battling cancer and undergoing chemotherapy, could only be dropped off by my aunt without any visitors allowed. None of this was normal, so it's essential to extend grace to those around you. Although the pandemic has officially ended, the lingering effects of COVID can still be felt today.

■ 2020: The Year the World Stopped - Reader Reflection

What did the pandemic teach you about yourself, your family, or what really matters?

The Significance of Socializing and Networking

Don't hold yourself back! In the world of entrepreneurship, mastering socializing and networking is crucial. Throughout my journey, I've gained invaluable insights and fostered connections with remarkable individuals.

- I've learned about marketing, content creation, and how to pinpoint my audience and niche.
- These connections have not only bolstered my business efforts but have also facilitated my personal growth on a spiritual level.
- I've even nurtured friendships that have evolved into family bonds across the United States.

A heartfelt thank you goes out to my coaches past and present, including Remiah Trask, Vernica Pitcher, CJ, Shi Cobb-Consulting, Tina Payne, and LaQueda Ricks. A very special thank you and shout-out to my licensed professional counselor/therapist D.Crockett. She is the best. She has truly help me navigate different phases in my life and is truly an inspiration. I also want to extend my gratitude to all my family, friends, and customers who have provided unwavering support throughout my business ventures. While I can't name everyone, please know that I truly appreciate you.

◼ The Significance of Socializing and Networking - Reader

Who is one person or connection that has shaped your journey in a meaningful way?

_____

_____

_____

Longing For More

In my late 30s, I noticed old emotions starting to resurface. A profound longing emerged within me, as if a void existed that I couldn't quite fill. Even though I possessed everything I wanted and needed, something still felt like it was missing. Watching television shows that depict the relationship between mothers and daughters stirred certain emotions, prompting me to question why I didn't have that bond with my mom.

I often found myself pondering why I wasn't raised alongside my siblings. This subject had never been broached with me, nor had I ever taken the initiative to discuss it.

One day, I decided to reach out to a life coach I admired for guidance. To my surprise, she informed me that she couldn't assist with my plans until I addressed my past. She suggested therapy and provided a contact. Oh my goodness, this turned out to be the best decision I ever made! My therapist is incredible; she listens attentively and assigns me tasks to work on. She keeps me accountable. I'm grateful to the life coach for her honesty about the journey I needed to undertake.

■ Longing for More - Reader Reflection

Is there a part of your past you've been avoiding but know you need to face? What would healing that part open up for your future?

Starting the Healing Process

During my therapy session, I opened up to my therapist about experiencing a sense of abandonment, and I was uncertain why these feelings had surfaced as I approached my 40s. After exploring my concerns, my assignment was to confront these emotions directly. I was encouraged to reach out to my mother in person rather than through text, express how I felt, and seek answers to my questions. This proved to be quite challenging. Each time I intended to ask, I struggled to find the right words, leading me to miss the opportunity once again.

Finally, one day, I shared my feelings with someone else, who then conveyed my message. I spoke with my mom, and she took the time to explain everything to me. My questions were answered, and I felt a sense of closure. This year marked a memorable occasion as I shared my birthday with my mom, my sibling, and my aunts. It was truly a joyful celebration.

Let me clarify, I have never held any anger towards my parents. I understand they were young when they had me and were doing their best for my well-being at that time. I hold the utmost respect for both of them and love them deeply. Mom and Dad, if you happen to be reading this, please do not feel any guilt this was all part of God's plan. He specifically chose you to be my parents, allowing me to come into this world to fulfill a mission and purpose.

■ Starting the Healing Process - Reader Reflection

What's one conversation you need to have with a loved one to gain peace or closure?

The Breakdown

Have you ever given your all 1,000% at work? Long hours spent laboring, often prioritizing work over time with your child or family. The stress of wanting everything to be perfect and correct. Staying up until 3 a.m., only to rise again at 6 a.m. I was running myself into the ground. Stress, anxiety, and depression can take a toll on you.

One day, my body finally gave out. I woke up gasping, feeling like I was choking. I couldn't breathe, swallow, or cough, and I thought I was dying. My life flashed before my eyes, and all I could utter was, "Lord, please help me." I wondered if this was what people feel when taking their last breath. It felt like the end was near.

Just then, as I cried out for help, I felt a sudden relief I could breathe again. I managed to cough and kept repeating, "Thank you, Jesus." At that moment, I had to throw up, and thankfully, my daughter heard me and came to assist. After that experience, with every breath I took, I expressed gratitude to the Lord. We often take for granted the simple act of breathing.

When I shared my ordeal with a few people, I learned it was a panic attack an experience I had never encountered before. I knew others who faced similar challenges, but I never thought I would be one of them. Following that episode, I took a three-month leave from work, which was essential for my recovery.

When I returned, I felt revitalized and had a fresh perspective on life. This serves as a friendly reminder to prioritize your physical, spiritual, and mental well-being. That job will remain, and the work will always be there; however, remember that if you were to pass away today or tomorrow, your position could be filled the very next day. Make sure to carve out time for yourself.

The Clock Stopped In July

At 3 AM, my phone began to ring incessantly. When I finally answered, it was my aunt urging me to get to the emergency room because my grandfather might have had a heart attack. Without hesitation, I jumped up, got dressed, made a few calls, gathered my daughter, and headed to the hospital. Upon arrival, the doctor informed me that it was a life-or-death situation. We had two choices: transfer him to another hospital for surgery, or he would not survive. He had an aortic dissection, a serious condition involving a tear in the wall of the aorta, the main artery carrying blood from the heart. As the tear extends, blood can flow between the layers of the vessel wall, leading to a dissection (MedlinePlus).

For 48 hours, my grandfather had kept his chest pains to himself. It was nothing short of a miracle that he was still with us. As they prepared him for transfer, I left to reach the other hospital first, ready to assist with registration and paperwork. When he arrived, I prayed with him, and it was time for surgery. The procedure lasted around six hours.

While we waited in the family room, the doctor finally came to us with troubling news: they had to go back in because he was bleeding again. Thankfully, it turned out to be just one stitch. They managed to repair the tear and save his life. After surgery, he was moved to the Critical Care Unit and then to rehab. My family and I stood by him every step of the way.

Being a caregiver during this challenging time was incredibly demanding, especially while trying to balance work. However, my family and I persevered as a team. My grandfather successfully completed rehab and returned home, resuming his usual activities. Now, he shares his testimony with everyone.

Slow Down, November

Every November, we plan a family vacation. The previous year, we spent our time in the scenic mountains of Tennessee. Last year, we opted to take the kids to Universal Studios, which was a blast, especially since it was my first visit. We enjoyed delicious meals, indulged in shopping, and explored multiple parks.

As our trip came to an end, we began our journey home. I started to feel overheated during the ride back and didn't think much of it. Once we reached Louisiana, I felt terrible. It began with chills, quickly followed by a fever. So, off to urgent care I went. Upon arrival, my temperature was 102°F. They conducted tests for the Flu, Strep, and COVID, all of which returned negative. They prescribed medication for my fever and body aches and sent me home.

The next day, I visited my primary care provider. The nurse mentioned that if the test beeps quickly, it indicates an issue. Just as she turned to leave, the machine went haywire. Despite feeling miserable, I couldn't help but laugh. She exclaimed, "Ma'am, what on earth were you doing? You have both the FLU and COVID!" All I could say was, "Traveling." Oh my, I felt like I was on the brink of death; it was an awful experience.

Throughout the entire pandemic, I managed to avoid getting sick. I consistently wore masks sometimes even two at a time and kept a supply of Lysol spray, wipes, and hand sanitizers on hand. Just when I finally relaxed and let down my guard, I fell ill. All I could do was try to rest and pray. I'm grateful to have made it through both illnesses. I know firsthand that COVID has taken many lives, and the FLU can be equally devastating.

I Speak Life! You Can't Have My Child

Life can often take unexpected turns. This was especially true in January 2023 when I faced a terrifying moment I nearly lost my child due to uncontrolled bleeding. By the time we arrived at Children's Hospital, she was so weak that we needed a wheelchair to get her inside. I can still picture her face; she appeared so pale.
As soon as we arrived, the medical team quickly took her vitals and initiated IV fluids.

I sensed the gravity of the situation when she remained silent, which was unusual for her, as she typically had a playful response to discussions about needles or blood draws. The hematologists soon came in to begin their assessment. I glanced at the monitor and saw her blood pressure was critically low, around 89/58, with a heart rate of 145. After their evaluation, they transferred us to the hematology unit, where we initially believed we would stay for just one day before being released.

In her situation, however, the circumstances were quite serious; her lab results indicated critically low levels. She needed two blood transfusions along with various medications to manage the bleeding. To make matters worse, her IVs repeatedly failed, requiring assistance from specialized teams. My child became increasingly frustrated with being confined to bed and frequently disturbed for medications, lab tests, and assessments. I could feel how disheartening this experience was for her, particularly as a teenager. She wasn't eating, was losing weight, and appeared quite downcast.

Every day, I made an effort to brighten her mood. We shared some lighthearted moments, with her teasingly attempting to direct me and claiming I was a poor nurse for not adhering to her "orders." *LOL!*

One morning, I awoke, placed my hands on her, and prayed, "Lord, please heal my child from the top of her head to the soles of her feet. Break every chain that holds her and any curses spoken against her; heal her in Jesus' name, Amen." I began bringing her food from outside, and soon after, she started receiving visitors daily. She grew stronger, and by day five, her lab results showed improvement, which led to our discharge. I am incredibly grateful to Children's Hospital in Baton Rouge; from the Emergency Room to the Hematology department, everyone was so supportive and treated us wonderfully... no complaints.

While on the Hematology unit, I had the opportunity to see some of the other children in the hospital, which reminded me of my godson Ziggy and his mother, Dominique. Tragically, Ziggy passed away in 2018 from leukemia. He had such a bright spirit, always smiling and laughing.

I reflected on how they must have felt during those long days and nights in Memphis at St. Jude, dealing with all the doctors and medications. The sleepless nights worrying while your child rests, wondering if everything would be alright. I pray for all the parents and families of ill children around the world. I pray for peace and the strength to endure during tough times. It will get better.

■ I Speak Life! You Can't Have My Child - Reader Reflection

When have you prayed or spoken life over someone you love? How did it strengthen your faith?

The Rebirth

I vividly recall standing at the front of my church as a young girl, surrounded by about ten of my cousins and friends, proclaiming our belief in Jesus and our desire to be baptized. While we sang about God and were aware of his existence, did we truly grasp the depth of what we were saying? Did we understand his grace, mercy, and love?

Reflecting on all the experiences I've encountered throughout my life, I can confidently affirm that God is real. He has sustained me during times when I could have lost my life or my sanity. Each morning, I am blessed with new grace and mercy, providing me another opportunity to navigate this journey called life and to make things right. I am incredibly grateful that he does not treat me as my sins deserve.

I recognize that we all practice different religions and may worship God in various ways, but ultimately, we serve one God. My belief in Jesus Christ is unwavering, and nothing can separate me from the love of God not even life or death. I made the decision to rededicate my life to Christ, and this time, it felt deeply personal. I forged my own relationship with God, having finally faced trials and tests that helped me understand what my grandparents and great-grandparents had spoken about.

On September 23, 2023, I was baptized at Rosehill Church, also known as "The Hill," by Pastor Danny Donaldson, where "practical teaching produces powerful living."

Redeemed, Renewed, Restored

I have been a member of Rosehill since 2015, and during this time, I have experienced significant growth and learning. This place is my spiritual home, and I find joy in serving and fulfilling my purpose. My involvement in the healthcare ministry is particularly rewarding.

I encourage you to seek out a church home where you can grasp and appreciate the teachings. Establish a personal relationship with God, as we will each be accountable for our own lives when we leave this world. No one be it mom, dad, or grandma can answer for you.
I hope this book inspires everyone and provides hope along with a fresh perspective on life.

Remember, trials and tests come to strengthen us. Keep pushing forward and don't give up; you will emerge victorious in the end. If no one else has told you this, I believe in you. You are more than a conqueror through Jesus. Embrace the life-changing power of healing. Be blessed!

◾ Redeemed, Renewed, Restored

What does redemption, renewal, and restoration look like in your life right now? Where have you seen God redeem your past, renew your spirit, or restore what was once broken?

"I survived the pain. I embraced the healing. Now, I'm living the rebirth."

You see the beauty, but not the ashes.
The home, the career, the businesses, the smile it all looks perfect from the outside.
But behind the glow is a story of survival, loss, and rebirth.

In I Survived It: The Rebirth, Chanel Landry takes you on an unfiltered journey through the triumphs and tragedies that shaped her life. From childhood innocence stolen, to the heartbreak of miscarriage, to the devastating loss of her beloved grandmother every page is a testament to the strength it takes to keep going when life breaks you down.

Through faith, forgiveness, and fierce determination, Chanel found the courage to rise again. She built a career as a nurse, became an entrepreneur, and most importantly reclaimed her voice and her healing. With raw honesty and unwavering faith, she invites you to walk with her through the valleys and witness how God's grace can transform pain into purpose.

This is more than a memoir its a guided journal. It is a message of hope for anyone who has faced trauma, grief, or betrayal and wondered if they could ever stand whole again. You can. You will. You shall.

Because survival is only the beginning, rebirth is where the real story begins.

Chanel Landry, BSN,RN, is a compassionate nurse with over 20 years of experience serving patients and families. A proud mother of one and an active member of her church's healthcare team, Chanel has dedicated her life to caring for others.

When she is not working or serving in ministry, Chanel finds joy in traveling, creating precious memories with family and friends, and embracing new adventures. Her love for people and her eye for fashion inspired her to entrepreneurial journey as founder of **Nola Scrubs®**, a medical scrub uniform boutique,: **Paris and Paisley Boutique,** women and children fashion brand; and **Rising Beyond Scars** a nonprofit organization devoted to helping others heal and grow.

Through her career, businesses, and her writing, Chanel continues to inspire others with her resilience, faith, and determination proving that even in life's hardest seasons, trials can be transformed into triumphs.